THE TWINS OF HOLLOW HOUSE

Written by Sana Rasoul
Illustrated by Dan Whisker

hachette
LEARNING

ISBN: 9781036000585

Text © Sana Rasoul
Design, illustrations and layout © 2025 Hodder & Stoughton Limited
First published in 2025 by Hachette Learning,
An Hachette UK Company
Carmelite House, 50 Victoria Embankment, London EC4Y 0DZ

www.HachetteLearning.com
The authorised representative in the EEA is Hachette Ireland, 8 Castlecourt Centre, Dublin 15, D15 XTP3, Ireland (email: info@hbgi.ie)

Impression number 10 9 8 7 6 5 4 3 2 1
Year 2029 2028 2027 2026 2025

Author: Sana Rasoul
Illustrator: Dan Whisker/The Bright Agency
Series Editor: Catherine Coe
Educational Consultant: Pauline Allen
Page layout: Rocket Design (East Anglia) Ltd

With thanks to the schools that took part in the development of *Reading Planet Cosmos*, including: Ancaster CE Primary School, Ancaster; Downsway Primary School, Reading; Ferry Lane Primary School, London; Foxborough Primary School, Slough; Griffin Park Primary School, Blackburn; St Barnabas CE First & Middle School, Pershore; Tranmoor Primary School, Doncaster; and Wilton CE Primary School, Wilton.

The Publishers would like to thank the following for permission to reproduce copyright material. Design: © tutti frutti/stock.adobe.com; © thongchainak/stock.adobe.com; © frilled dragon/stock.adobe.com; © Alex/stock.adobe.com; © Allusioni/stock.adobe.com

All rights reserved. Apart from any use permitted under UK copyright law, no part of this publication may be reproduced or transmitted in any form or by any means, electronic or mechanical, including photocopying and recording, or held within any information storage and retrieval system, without permission in writing from the publisher or under licence from the Copyright Licensing Agency Limited. Further details of such licences (for reprographic reproduction) may be obtained from the Copyright Licensing Agency Limited, www.cla.co.uk

A catalogue record for this title is available from the British Library.

Printed in the UK

Hachette UK's policy is to use papers that are natural, renewable and recyclable products and made from wood grown in sustainable forests and other controlled sources. The logging and manufacturing processes are expected to conform to the environmental regulations of the country of origin.

To order please visit www.HachetteLearning.com or contact Customer Service at education@hachette.co.uk / +44 (0)1235 827827

Contents

1. The Big Move 4
2. Unwelcomed 11
3. Monsters 18
4. Missing 28
5. Hide and Seek 34
6. The Basement 45
7. The Battle for Hollow House 59
8. Farewell 64

The Big Move

Deshty paused outside the towering house, too stunned to move. She slipped the backpack off her shoulder and turned to her brother.

"I told you," Darian moaned, "it looks even creepier in real life."

Hollow House looked like someone had picked it up by the roots, dipped it in tar and placed it back in Cemetery Grove.

"Darian? Deshty? Your dad is here. Come and help with the boxes," Mum shouted from behind them as the removal van came to a halt.

Darian kicked the parched grass in frustration, sending small pieces of rock flying in the air.

"Stop that!" Deshty shouted. "It's not as bad as you're making out."

"I hate this place," Darian mumbled miserably as he shuffled towards the van.

Deshty didn't follow. Their drive to Cemetery Grove had been long, and her ears were still ringing from her brother's never-ending whinging. She'd barely said a word from the excitement. She was used to plain old houses that all looked the same, but Hollow House was different. She smiled to herself as she thought about the hidden treasures she might find inside.

"Why aren't you helping your brother?" Frowning, Mum appeared by her side.

Fascinated, Deshty couldn't peel her eyes away from the house. It was the crumbling roof she noticed first. Yellow ivy snaked up the chipped turret like hungry tentacles. The windows were large and wide but smudged with dirt and stained by time.

"We'll give the place a nice makeover," her mum said cheerfully, "and thanks to its cheap price, we'll have a bit of extra cash to spend doing it up."

Deshty opened her mouth to say something, but the words got all jumbled up in her brain, so she swallowed them instead.

Her brother was the talkative one, not her. Whenever anybody found out she was a twin, they always told her how amazing it must be. Except, it *wasn't*. Apart from having the same dark hair, brown eyes and eyelashes that flicked towards the sky, she and Darian were different in every other way.

"Can I get the biggest room?" Deshty asked.

"Every room is big here!" Mum said cheerfully. "Come on, let's get you inside."

"I'll be there in a second," Deshty promised.

It only took another glance at Hollow House for Deshty to be certain of this: no one had lived here for a long time. She could tell by the way the house stood, surrounded by rotting plants and patches of yellowing grass. Deshty glanced backwards nervously. She had the strangest feeling someone was watching her, but she shook it off as nervous excitement and walked into the house.

From inside, Hollow House was bigger than she'd expected, with three bedrooms, a library, a piano room and a basement. Deshty was surprised by all the stuff already in the house. The previous owners must have left it behind.

Strange, Deshty thought.

She walked around the ground floor, poking her head into all the rooms until she stood outside the basement door. She tried the handle, but it was locked. Deshty peered through the keyhole, hoping to see a glimpse of what was inside. A flash of electric blue light nearly blinded her. She jumped on the spot, her heart pumping. Taking a deep breath, Deshty looked again, but now the light was gone, and the room was pitch-black. It must have been the sunlight pouring in from a window, she thought, maybe reflecting off something blue.

Giving up on the basement, Deshty went up to find her bedroom. Stale air drifted from the cracks in the floorboards as she climbed up the stairs. Everything creaked and cracked, like brittle bones. In the shadowy corners of the house, cobwebs clung to the ceiling for dear life.

She found her cluttered room, full of boxes her dad had brought up and patterned floral furniture that wasn't theirs.

Outside her room, Deshty heard a loud crash followed by clumsy footsteps. She ran to the door and stuck her head out.

"Darian? Is that you?"

Silence.

"You're not funny," she yelled.

When Deshty heard nothing back, she took a few tentative steps forward and noticed a large painting hanging lopsided at the top of the stairs. Deshty walked towards it, reached up on her tiptoes and straightened the frame. Pleased with herself, she took a step back and looked at the painting carefully. It was of Hollow House, exactly as it was now but without the crumbling roof. She didn't know why, but it creeped her out. The house in the picture looked dark and unfriendly — almost menacing.

Deshty reached out to touch the painting when a loud knock from down the corridor stopped her. Deshty felt something warm brush against her shoulder.

Slowly, she turned around and saw a monster standing in front of her. The creature had cracked skin, sharp teeth and sunken eyes that glowered at her emotionlessly.

Deshty's scream echoed throughout the house.

"Gotcha!" the monster said. It took her a couple of seconds to realise it was not an actual monster, but her brother.

"You should have seen your face! That's one-nil to me," Darian said, mimicking her scream.

Unwelcomed

"Where did you get that thing from?" Scowling, she pulled the mask off her brother's face.

"I found it just now, in one of the cupboards downstairs," he said.

"Ergh!" She threw the mask away in disgust and walked back into her room. The stuffy summer heat was uncomfortable, making sweat drip down her back, so she kept the door to her room slightly ajar and the windows wide open. Deshty could spot Darian hovering outside her door, his shadow moving back and forth. The floorboards rattled from the weight of his stamping feet.

"Go away!" she yelled.

Her bedroom door slammed shut with a loud bang.

"I'm going to—" Deshty swung open the door but there was no sign of her brother.

Confused, she searched for Darian in the corridor before going into his room, right opposite hers, but he wasn't there either.

It was only when she leaned over the railing that she saw he was downstairs, with Mum and Dad. Odd – she could have sworn she'd seen a shadow moving outside her door. Deshty couldn't face going back into her boiling room, so she spent the rest of the day helping her parents unpack downstairs until it was time to sleep. Thankfully, her room had a cool breeze to it by then.

*****

Early the next morning, Deshty was jolted awake by a disturbing sound. Someone was on the roof. Patter. Patter. Patter. Wiping the sleep from her eyes, she got out of bed and pressed her face against the window. It was impossible to see the roof from where she was standing. She tried the other window, but still, her view of the roof was obstructed. She turned round to the sound of her door flying open, Dad barging into the room. His hair was dishevelled, and his eyes were barely the size of two peas.

"Deshty! Can you stop making so much noise? Last night was bad enough. Your room is directly above ours!" he grunted.

"Huh? Last night? I never made any noise …"

"And just now? What have you been doing to cause such a racket?"

"I've only just woken up!" Deshty protested.

"You have?" He looked at her in surprise.

The hairs on the back of Deshty's neck stood alert.

"Never mind then – it must have been a mouse or squirrel or something," Dad said, reading her mind. "Now we're both up, come down and I'll make you some breakfast. I think I heard Darian getting up too."

After a hearty plate of warm fluffy bread and perfectly cooked eggs, Deshty decided to join her brother outside.

It was too hot indoors and her parents were busy getting their catering business up and running again, after the move.

When she stepped out into the garden, Deshty was surprised by how quiet it was. She was used to hearing all sorts of sounds – the neighbour's lawnmower going off, or the screeching of birds overhead. Hollow House sat on its own, like an island yet to be inhabited. Darian was by the edge of the garden, waving a tree branch in the air. The garden looked wild, full of trees and bushes with a slight slope going downhill. Spotting an opportunity to get her own back, Deshty slowed down her pace until she was right behind Darian.

Deshty tapped him on both shoulders and roared as loudly as she could in his ear.

"Argh! Don't do that!" he yelled, a nervous edge to his voice.

"You do it to me all the time!" she argued back. "What are you doing out here anyway?"

"I'm collecting sticks — Dad said if I get enough of them, we can have a bonfire night."

"He only said that to trick you into tidying the garden," she told him. "Didn't you learn your lesson from the time he made you clear the attic back home?"

Darian looked down at the branch in his hand before flinging it across the garden.

"I can't believe I fell for that," he said.

"You need to cheer up," Deshty said. "Remember what Dad told us? We can get a pool once he saves up enough money." But not even the possibility of an outdoor pool brought a smile to Darian's face, so Deshty tried something else.

"Do you want to explore the house? There are still rooms we haven't looked at properly."

"What's there to see?" Darian sulked.

"Lots of things!" Deshty explained. "I only had a quick look yesterday, and some of the rooms were locked," she added, remembering the basement.

"I guess," Darian replied. "It's not like I've got anything better to do. We've got no Wi-Fi until next week."

It wasn't the most enthusiastic response, but Deshty was glad that her brother was going to join her. It wasn't as fun exploring things on your own.

"If we find anything good, who gets to keep it?" Darian asked, and Deshty found herself smiling at that. As much as she hated to admit it, there was never a dull moment when her brother was around.

"We could take it in turns," she suggested. "Let's start with the library."

3

Monsters

The library was a grand, formal room, positioned at the back of the house. There was marble flooring, expensive looking tables and shelves stuffed full of dusty old books. Entire rows of books greeted Deshty as she brushed her fingers against the spines. She couldn't believe so many things had been left behind in the house. Why would the people who lived here before them not take any of it?

Deshty walked up and down the aisles of books, feeling restless and on edge. The light switch wasn't working, and the towers of books blocked the sunlight from coming in through the windows. There were small photo frames hanging on the wall – more pictures of Hollow House. In the corner of a black and white photo were two figures. They were shrouded in darkness so she couldn't see their faces.

One figure was as tall and thin as a lamppost, and the other short and round.

"Look at this picture – who do you think they are? Maybe they lived here before …" Deshty turned to her brother, but he wasn't there. Confused, she looked over her shoulder to see where he'd gone. He couldn't have got bored already.

"Darian, where are you?" she shouted.

No answer.

Shaking her head, Deshty put the frame back where she found it and went in search of her brother. When she was halfway down one of the aisles, her attention diverted to a book poking out of the shelf, titled *Hollow House*. Curious, she picked it off the shelf and turned to the first page, but it was blank. Deshty flipped the pages and realised they were all blank except for a rushed scribble at the bottom of the last page.

'Get out before it's too late', someone had written.

Frowning, she stared at the book in a trance. Suddenly, a noise to her left made her jump in shock and the book fell from her hands.

One by one, entire rows of books tumbled to the floor.

The noise echoed around the room and filled her ears. Deshty breathed heavily and her palms felt sweaty. From the corner of her eye, she noticed a slight flicker of movement – a flash of skin.

Peering through the small gap of the books, she found herself staring at a bony face with large wide-set eyes that flashed with trickery. The figure raised one hand in the air, revealing long yellow talons. The hand reached out towards her. Deshty ran – so fast, she thought her legs were going to come off.

She slipped on the marble floor then picked herself up again only to bump headfirst into Darian by the door.

"Ouch! Watch where you're going!" He rubbed his temple. "What happened here? Why are all the books on the floor?" he asked, pointing behind her.

Darian's voice flooded Deshty with momentary relief, but as she stared at him, her eyes widened with realisation. She clutched her heart and laughed out loud. Of course! It must have been Darian she'd seen just then – not a monster at all!

"That was a good one," she laughed even harder. "Let me guess – you found another stinky mask in the house."

"What are you talking about?" Darian narrowed his eyes.

"Just now with the mask, and the note in the book? Nice touch." She had to hand it to him – he knew how to get her heart pumping.

"I have no clue what you're talking about."

"Yeah, okay sure! So where were you then? Did you go and put the mask on?"

Her brother frowned.

"Did you see someone in here?" he said.

"You didn't answer my question. Where were you if it wasn't you I saw just now?" Deshty wasn't going to make it easy on him.

"I heard music coming from the other room so I went to check it out. I thought it might be Mum or Dad playing music but when I opened the door, the music just stopped."

Unsure whether Darian was messing with her again, she decided to call his bluff.

"Show me," she said.

Deshty followed her brother out to the piano room opposite the library.

As she reached for the doorknob, Deshty heard a melody coming from inside the room.

She froze. Someone *was* playing the piano.

"See! I told you," Darian whispered.

When she opened the door, the room fell silent. The piano was sitting in the centre of the room, surrounded by music sheets. The sheets were everywhere — on top of the piano and scattered all over the floor.

Deshty stared at her brother.

"You heard the music, right? I wasn't lying." He stared at the empty stool in front of the piano.

"There's no one here." She pointed out the obvious.

"No one we can see," Darian said.

"You're being silly!" Deshty laughed.

"Then how do you explain what just happened?" he said, challenging her with his eyes.

"Well, Dad said we might have mice so it was probably one of them running over the keys."

Her brother turned pale.

"A m-m-mouse!" he repeated.

"Don't start panicking," Deshty said, forgetting her brother had a deep fear of mice and rats. "Were you really here the whole time?" she asked.

"I did follow you into the library but I left when I heard the music."

Deshty bit her lip. Darian could have heard the music playing *after* he'd tried to scare her. The alternative was too disturbing to think about.

"Let me have a go at playing." Deshty sat down on the piano stool. She had never played the piano before. How hard could it be? Deshty made a show of raising her hands in the air but as she was about to press down on the keys, the piano screeched, lifting off the ground for a moment. She fell from the stool and scrambled to her feet in panic.

"D-did you see that?" she yelled.

Darian opened his mouth but no words came out.

Deshty tried to come up with a logical reason for the piano moving on its own, but she could think of absolutely nothing. All the windows were closed, so it couldn't have been a breeze. Even if they had been open, no amount of wind could have moved the piano that far across the room.

"Let's get out of here," Darian said, his voice barely a squeak.

"Good idea," she said, turning to leave the room.

Mum appeared by the door.

"What was that noise?" Mum looked at them suspiciously.

"Oh! Are you both making use of the piano? I still can't believe our luck — someone just left it behind!"

Lucky? Deshty didn't feel so lucky, not anymore.

"I've got to get back to work but I'm going to need your help clearing up at some point. Look at all this dust ..." Mum waved her hands in the air and left the room.

Deshty and Darian followed behind.

"Why didn't you tell her about the piano moving?" Darian whispered.

"We don't even know what happened," she said, trying to sound calm but her heart was still racing in her chest. "Tell me the truth. Did you try to scare me in the library earlier?"

Darian shook his head, looking puzzled.

"It really wasn't me!"

Deshty couldn't deny it now — this confirmed her suspicion. The scary face she'd seen in the library had been real!

"I've got to find that book!" she mumbled.

"What book? What happened in there anyway?"

Deshty turned and ran back into the library but when she opened the door, she gasped in disbelief.

The books were lined up neatly on the shelves again, as if she had imagined the entire thing. As Deshty stared at the library, totally confused, Darian appeared behind her. "Mum must've tidied up when we were in the piano room," he said, looking around him. "What are you looking for?"

"That book'... I think someone hid it here to warn us," she told him.

"What did it say?"

Deshty almost didn't want to tell him.

"Get out before it's too late," she said shakily.

The creature she'd seen hadn't been reaching for her, she realised. It had been trying to take the book.

Missing

That afternoon, Deshty couldn't stop thinking about what had happened. She replayed the events in the library over and over again in her mind, but she couldn't come up with a less terrifying explanation. The monster she'd seen was real. Darian was unusually quiet too, sticking to Mum and Dad like glue as they worked in the kitchen. In the evening, Deshty decided to tackle the task of unpacking her things. It would take her mind off the strange events of the day.

She started with her small suitcase, taking out the clothes and folding them carefully on the bed. She turned to grab the larger suitcase, but it wasn't in the room. Weird – Deshty was sure she'd seen her dad bring it up earlier.

Deshty got up and walked into her brother's room, where an eerie silence met her. She switched on the light, and a faint glow bathed the entire room. Her suitcase wasn't here either. Maybe her dad had taken it back down for some reason, she thought as she walked back into her room.

When she turned to face the bed, Deshty noticed that her clothes had vanished. The very ones she had just folded! Confused, Deshty looked around her when she heard a thumping sound coming from inside the wardrobe. She screamed as loudly as she could.

Footsteps boomed up the stairs and Dad came bursting through the door.

"What is it, honey? What happened?" he said, out of breath and pink in the face. His eyes filled with worry when he saw her expression.

"I-I ... I just folded my clothes on my bed and now they're all gone. I think something is inside there." She pointed to the wardrobe.

Dad gave her a quizzical look before marching to the wardrobe. He opened the door, poked his head inside and re-emerged with a frown on his face.

"Are you sure you didn't just misplace the clothes? There's nothing in there ..."

"I didn't misplace them!" she insisted. "I can't find my suitcase either – the big one. Didn't you bring it up here earlier?"

"Possibly, but I've been up and down these stairs so many times today I couldn't tell you, love. It'll be in the house somewhere."

Mum and Darian appeared at the doorway.

"What's wrong, sweetie?"

"It's nothing," Deshty said. It wasn't like her mum would

believe her if her dad hadn't about the clothes going missing.

There was an awkward pause when no one really said anything.

"We're just going to be downstairs, sweetheart, okay?" her dad finally said, giving her shoulder a squeeze.

He walked out of the room with Mum by his side. They began whispering earnestly before disappearing down the stairs.

Darian lingered in the room. Deshty didn't say anything – he would only make a joke out of it, and that was the last thing Deshty wanted to hear right now.

Instead, her brother closed her door and turned to face her. The seriousness in his eyes took her by surprise – Darian was rarely serious about anything.

"I heard what you said to Dad earlier. Is it true? Did your stuff just disappear?"

"Stop eavesdropping on me!" she lashed out at him, not knowing how else to deal with her rollercoaster of emotions. "And before you say anything—"

"The same thing happened to me," Darian interrupted. "Some of my stuff isn't where I put it." He spoke quickly and quietly.

"Are you serious?" Deshty asked, half relieved to know she wasn't the only one this was happening to. It was selfish of her, but she couldn't help it.

Darian pulled out a book from underneath his hoody.

"Is this the book you saw in the library?" He showed her the last page.

Deshty swallowed the lump in her throat.

"Where'd you find it?" she asked him.

"It was on my bed, open on this page! I tried explaining to Mum and Dad but they didn't believe me. They think I wrote it as a joke," Darian said. "The house is haunted, isn't it?"

Deshty shook her head.

"No, I don't think it's ghosts doing this ..." A flashback of the library ran through her mind. "*Monsters* ..." she said slowly.

Biting his nails, Darian sat down on the bed. "Monsters?" he repeated, the colour had drained from his face.

"Earlier in the library, I saw this ... creature." Deshty didn't know how else to explain what it was – all she was sure of was that it wasn't human.

"What did it look like?" Darian asked.

"It had leathery grey skin, huge eyes and sharp nails." She wrapped her arms around her chest and told Darian everything that had happened earlier that day. When she finished talking, Darian buried his face in his hands.

"What do we do now?" he said. "It's not like we can leave the house – we only just moved in!"

"We have to figure this out together, in secret," Deshty said. She couldn't help but feel a small thrill rush through her. What exactly would they find next?

5

Hide and Seek

A fierce gust of wind swept through the morning air and rattled Deshty's bedroom window. She rolled over in bed and pulled the cover over her head. The howls of the wind turned into angry knocking, and when thunder finally erupted, Deshty sat bolt upright. Thunder in the middle of summer? What was going on?

"Deshty! Deshty! Come here, quickly!"

It was Darian, and he sounded desperate. She flung the door open and ran into her brother's room. He stood by the window with a pair of binoculars in his hands.

"What is it?" she asked, looking out of the window.

"Here." He pressed the binoculars into her hand. "Over there by the tree – can you see that thing?"

She lifted the binoculars to her eyes and saw a flash of grey disappearing behind the shed. Her blood froze.

"Keep looking," Darian said.

For a split second, the grey creature came into full view. It was smaller and pudgier than the monster she'd seen in the library, but with the same leathery skin. Its eyes were so large they covered half its face. The binoculars slipped from her sweaty hands.

"Did you see what it was carrying?" Darian asked.

Deshty nodded.

"Clothes and toys," she said quietly. "I think it's our missing stuff." When she finally mustered the courage to look again, the monster had vanished.

"Should we go down and check?" Deshty said, but Darian remained quiet. "Though if you're too scared …"

"I'm not scared!" Darian interjected.

"Then let's go to the garden and see if we can find some of our stuff," she insisted.

Still in their pyjamas, they headed down the stairs, ignoring Mum beckoning them to have breakfast.

Deshty walked quickly, telling herself that nothing was going to happen to her in broad daylight. The sun was shining again and her parents were just inside. It was going to be okay.

"Behind there." Darian pointed to the shed.

She crept closer, blood rushing to her face. Taking a deep breath, Deshty leaned forward and put a hand to her mouth. Rushing to her side, Darian gawped at the pile of clothes and toys chucked carelessly on the ground.

They were torn up, dirty and broken.

"My stuff …" Darian said, picking up the broken drone Grandad had got him for his birthday. It was snapped in two. Deshty's favourite cherry-coloured jumper was torn at the sides. She looked at her brother and a light bulb switched on in her mind.

"Let's get Mum and Dad out here – they'll have to believe us when they see this."

"You're right!" Darian said.

They sprinted into the house, shouting at the top of their lungs.

"Mum! Dad!"

"They must be in the kitchen working," her brother said when no answer came, so they headed in that direction.

"Mum? Dad?" Deshty tried again.

"What is it?" her mum said from behind the kitchen counter.

"Please come to the garden. We need to show you something," Deshty said.

"Can't it wait? We're in the middle of work …" her dad grunted.

"No, it can't. Please! Hurry!" It was Darian who spoke now, his voice desperate and hopeful at the same time.

Reluctantly, Mum and Dad followed them to the garden. Deshty ran ahead, panting as she got to the shed.

"What are we looking at here?" Dad said impatiently.

"Our missing stuff is—" Deshty froze mid-sentence.

When she looked behind the shed, their stuff was gone – all evidence of the monster's existence vanished.

Darian looked at Deshty in disbelief.

"Where did it go?" he whispered.

"Well?" Mum said, tapping her foot on the ground.

Behind Mum's shoulder Deshty suddenly saw the round grey creature enter the house, but it spotted her too. Before it disappeared inside, it grinned at Deshty – an evil, malicious grin that made her skin tingle with an icy fear. She clutched her brother's arm and looked up at her parents.

"Over there!" she pointed. "It's in the house!"

Mum and Dad looked at each other.

"Who's inside, Deshty? You're worrying us!" Mum said.

"The monster," Darian blurted out.

"What?" Dad gave Darian and Deshty *the* look. The one they always got whenever they got caught in a lie.

"It's true – they're inside," Deshty insisted.

Dad opened his mouth to say something, but Mum put an arm on his shoulder to stop him. She shook her head and looked at Deshty.

"Your dad and I will have a look around whilst you both have breakfast, okay?"

They walked in together and waited anxiously as Mum and Dad searched the house. It didn't take long for them to join Deshty and Darian back in the kitchen.

"There's no one here," Dad started to say. "Don't forget, this is an old house and you've got an active imagination!" He looked at Deshty but she knew it wasn't her imagination that was running wild, it was the monsters!

"Yeah, that must be it," Deshty lied, realising their parents would never believe them, not if they couldn't prove it. It was up to her and Darian to figure this out.

"What now?" Darian said as soon as they left the kitchen.

"We have to find out everything there is to know about the house," she said. "We can look it up on Dad's tablet."

"How? We have no internet connection," her brother reminded her.

"We can ask Mum and Dad to take us to the local library — I saw one when we drove through on our way here and I bet they have WiFi."

"We've run out of some ingredients so I'm popping to the shops — do you two need anything?" Dad emerged from the kitchen.

"Actually, Dad, can we come with you? We want to go to the library for a bit," Deshty said.

"Yes, sure. Go and get ready quickly."

The sky had turned a moody grey, switching between bouts of sunshine and chilling winds as they drove to the town centre. Neither Deshty, nor her brother, said anything until they parked outside the library.

It wasn't a cheery building, with yellowing walls and a sulky librarian at the front desk.

"I'll be at the shops just down the road. Will you two be okay for a little while?" Dad asked.

Deshty nodded, and she and Darian wasted no time, quickly logging onto the library WiFi on their tablet. Deshty sat down and typed 'Hollow House, Cemetery Grove'. She could hear her own heart beating, and Darian's shallow breathing next to her ear. A list of articles appeared in the search engine, and she began scrolling through them.

"There!" Her brother pointed to the bottom of the page at an article titled 'The Mystery of Hollow House, Cemetery Grove'. "Read what it says."

11:20

The Mystery of Hollow House, Cemetery Grove

Everyone loves an urban myth, and we've uncovered a great one in the notorious town of Cemetery Grove. Steeped in mystery and folklore, Cemetery Grove has had its fair share of rumours. Last month, we uncovered the tale of Beastly Manor. This week, the spotlight is on Hollow House. Legend has it the house was once inhabited by a scheming pair known simply as Flesh and Bones.

The myth goes that Flesh and Bones wanted to isolate Hollow House from everything, and everyone. Residents blamed the evil creatures for cursing the house and unleashing their fury on anyone who dared to go anywhere near the place. Of course, there is no evidence to prove any of this is true, but some anonymous sources claim they've seen a blue current shooting up from the house. What this blue current is and what it signifies remains a well-kept secret.

FACT OR FICTION …

Our verdict?

FICTION!

It's a creepy story, but that's all it is, folks!

Next week, we explore the origins of the Loch Ness Monster in our FACT OR FICTION column.

"Flesh and Bones ..." Deshty whispered, "that's what they're called." The monster she saw in the library must have been Bones, and the one in the garden was Flesh. Goosebumps appeared up her arm. Pacing back and forth, Darian chewed the skin around his nails.

Deshty turned to the screen and read the article again but more slowly, in case she'd missed anything the first-time round.

"I wasn't imagining things!" she yelled out.

"What did you find?" Darian rushed to her side.

"The article mentions a blue current. I think I saw a flash of light in the basement but I couldn't get in because the door was locked."

Deshty's stomach did a somersault.

"You don't think Flesh and Bones live in the basement, do you?" Darian said.

"I'm not sure, but we've got to get down there and find out," Deshty decided.

"Should we tell Mum and Dad?" Darian asked.

Deshty shook her head. "They won't believe us even if we do – you heard them earlier!"

"But we can't go alone … what if they trap us there with them?" Darian's voice cracked as he spoke.

"We have no choice – it's the only room we haven't looked in and we might find something that will help us get rid of them."

"Fine," Darian said. "When do you want to go?"

"As soon as we get back," Deshty replied, afraid that she'd lose her courage if they waited any longer.

"There you two are!" Dad whispered from behind them. "Ready to go?"

They followed Dad out of the library and into the car. Deshty was glad when he turned the radio on full blast; it helped drown out the fearful beat of her heart and the busy chatter in her mind. Still, she was as cold as an ice lolly at the thought of what she and Darian might find in the basement.

6
The Basement

The sky was still full of sunshine when they arrived back at Hollow House. Deshty and Darian ran inside, waved a quick hello to Mum, and headed straight for the basement. They stood outside the door. It was still locked.

Deshty pushed against the door, but it wouldn't budge. She bent down towards the small gap between the door and filthy floor. Her nose was so close to the ground, she was practically inhaling the fluff and dust. Peering through the gap, flashes of blue light nearly blinded her. She staggered to her feet and beckoned Darian to look.

"Do you see the blue light? What is it?" she said quietly.

"Let me try something." Her brother looked around the room before his eyes settled on Deshty. "Give me that clip in your hair." He reached out his hand.

"Why?" she questioned.

"I think I can unlock the door. Uncle Karim showed me how when Dad last took us to see him."

Which is precisely why Mum doesn't like us going over there, Deshty thought.

She gave Darian the clip and, with a look of concentration on his face, he turned the sharp edge of the clip left then right until they both heard a soft CLICK.

Slowly, Darian opened the door. There was a set of stairs leading down to the basement, and a crackling sound coming from below them. Neither of them dared say anything as flashes of blue light filled the space below them, reminding Deshty of lightning in the dead of night.

Darian froze to the spot, so Deshty walked ahead of him. She tried to find a light switch but there was none.

"I don't think we should go down there," he whispered behind her.

"You stay here if you want, but I'm going!" Deshty wanted to know where the light was coming from. When she reached the bottom of the stairs, there was nothing but an endless ray of silvery blue light. It sent an Arctic chill through her bones. Her eyes adjusted to the constant firework of dancing sparks, until she saw a tiny hole in the middle of the floor. That was where all the light was shooting out from. It looked like a portal of some sort, but when she tried to get closer, the basement suddenly filled with darkness.

Deshty began to panic.

"Stop breathing on me!" she hissed, turning to face Darian, but it wasn't his hot stale breath she could feel on her skin.

Bones!

A startled Deshty backed away as she craned her neck to look up at Bones. He was so tall that his head nearly hit the ceiling. His silvery skin glowed in the dark and his fingers were thin and skeletal.

"Darian! Help!' she screamed, dodging Bone's outstretched hand. She ran up the stairs, but the basement door was shut. She rattled the door, desperate to get away from Bones but it wouldn't open. Deshty realised she was down there with the monster alone.

"Darian!" Frantic, she banged on the door as Bones stood at the bottom of the stairs.

"Leave!" he growled at her just as the door flung open to a red-faced Darian and a bewildered looking Dad.

"What are you doing down here?" Dad asked.

Deshty lunged forward, wrapping her arms around her dad – she'd never been more pleased to see him than in that very moment.

"Hey, look at me, sweetie. What's going on?"

"There's someone down there!" She pointed to the basement.

Dad sighed.

"You two are out to scare yourselves, aren't you? You shouldn't be in the basement."

"Please, just look," Deshty pleaded.

"Fine, I'll go and grab a torch but I'm sure I won't find anyone down there! This is the wardrobe all over again." Dad ushered them away from the basement, so they went and sat outside the house.

"What happened to you?" She turned to Darian. "You left me down there!"

"I ... I saw Flesh coming up the stairs. He came out of nowhere and then the door banged shut. I couldn't get it open, so I ran to get Dad."

"Flesh was there too?" Deshty said as her stomach churned.

"Did you see anything that could help us when you were down there?" Darian asked.

"Only Bones, and a hole in the ground where the blue light was coming from," she told him.

"A hole?"

"I was thinking," Deshty started, "they might be using that hole as some kind of portal to come in and out of the house when they want."

Darian looked deep in thought when the front door opened behind them.

"You'll be happy to know there's nothing in the basement," Dad said. "You two have enough imagination to fill up the world." Dad chuckled to himself and wandered back into the house. Deshty felt the disappointment deep in the pit of her stomach, like a heavy rock weighing her down.

"I know what we have to do," Darian said, his eyes gleamed bright against the deep blue evening sky.

"What?" she asked.

"We need to fill up that hole so they can't come up through it."

"Yes! That's a good idea," Deshty agreed. "Tomorrow morning when Mum and Dad are busy with work."

They stayed outside until Mum called them for dinner, but Deshty couldn't muster the energy to eat properly. When it was finally time to sleep, Deshty closed her eyes and tried to think of happy thoughts, but Flesh and Bones haunted her dreams.

The next morning, Deshty woke to a knock on the door.

"Are you up?" Darian said.

Kicking the duvet away, Deshty got up as Darian came into the room.

"I couldn't sleep," he said.

"Me neither." She rubbed her sore eyes.

"What are we going to fill that hole up with?" Darian asked her.

"Anything chunky or heavy ..." Deshty said.

"What about all those books in the library?" Darian suggested.

"That could work," she agreed.

"Deshty, Darian, come downstairs and have some breakfast!" Mum yelled.

Deshty picked at her food. She still had no appetite, and the smell of eggs made her feel sick. Her mum was a great cook, so Deshty knew it wasn't the food upsetting her stomach. Darian drank his juice without saying a word, leaving his plate untouched.

"Have you two seen my jewellery box? The one with the spinning ballerina on top?" Mum asked them.

Deshty turned to her brother but didn't dare say anything.

"I swear I feel like I'm so distracted lately – I can't find anything in this place!"

A small noise escaped Darian's lips.

"What was that, honey?" Mum said.

"Nothing. I'm not very hungry."

"Oh! I hope you're not getting sick?" Mum fussed.

"No, I'm fine."

"Okay, well, why don't you go and lie down for a bit? It's still early and your dad and I are very busy today with work."

"We should get a suitcase to carry books into the basement," Deshty said as they left the breakfast table.

"I'll go and get two empty ones from upstairs." Darian ran ahead of her. She waited in the library alone, a chilling cold running through her.

She couldn't help but look over her shoulder every couple of seconds. Her fears were developing wings of their own, flying around her in a dazed loop. Deshty licked her dry lips to give them some moisture and began piling the heaviest books on the floor in a neat stack. When Darian returned with two big suitcases, they started filling them up right away.

Satisfied that they had packed enough books to cover the hole, Deshty and Darian wheeled the suitcases past Mum, who was too busy chatting on the phone to notice them. Dad had his back to them when they passed the kitchen, as he hummed to the music coming out of the small speaker.

When they reached the basement door, Deshty wasn't surprised to find it was locked. She gave a hair clip to Darian, and he unlocked it whilst she kept a watchful eye out for signs of Flesh and Bones. Deshty expected to see the flashing blue lights once more, but it was dark and shadowy instead. Carefully, they dragged the suitcases down the stairs. Deshty winced at how loud the noise of the wheels were against the wooden steps, but Flesh and Bones were nowhere to be seen.

A small stream of light from the tiny window lit up the concrete floor, which had small cracks running along it. It reminded Deshty of the inside of an Egyptian pyramid from a documentary she'd seen. There were cases of light bulbs and other unlabelled boxes scattered all over the place.

Glancing nervously around him, Darian paused in the centre of the basement.

"Where's the hole?" he asked.

With one eye on the basement door above her, Deshty crouched low and ran her hands against the floor, looking for the hole in the ground. Maybe there was a secret button somewhere that opened the portal, Deshty thought. She searched again but couldn't find anything at all.

"Look at all this stuff," Darian said, peering at the open box to his left. He picked up a photo and showed it to her. "It's Flesh and Bones, look over here!" Darian pointed to the blurry figures next to the monsters. One was as tall and thin as a rod, with long white hair and eyes that covered most of its face. The other figure was wide and round. They smiled in the picture, revealing sharp canine teeth.

"This must be their mum and dad. I really thought our plan would work, but if we can't find the hole, we can't block it," Deshty said, feeling disappointed that it had come to nothing.

"Leave the suitcases here – we'll try again later," Darian said.

Just as they were about to leave, the door to the basement creaked open. Deshty looked up at a pair of gleaming eyes, folded grey skin and a bald head.

"Got you," Flesh hissed.

Deshty wanted to scream, but it was like her voice had grown legs and run away from her because it was nowhere to be found. She could feel Darian's fear as he gripped her arm, his fingers digging into her skin, and she drew in a big breath.

They were trapped.

They cowered in the corner, but as soon as Flesh started coming down the steps, a glittering flash of blue light emerged in the centre of the room. A small hole in the ground began to reveal itself.

"Quickly, dump the books in there," Deshty said, but Flesh was reaching for both suitcases. With one swift movement, he swung them across the basement.

Darian screamed.

"Leave our stuff! Leave this house!" Flesh growled as sparks of shooting light filled the basement.

The portal only shows itself when the monsters are in the basement, Deshty thought.

With her breath caught in her throat, Deshty tried to run up the stairs, but Flesh blocked her path. Darian threw his weight against Flesh, who wobbled on the spot from the impact. Deshty took the opportunity to push Flesh as hard as she could. He fell backwards into the hole but only a few seconds later the ground coughed Flesh back up into the basement with a stream of blue light.

He let out an injured wail.

"Let's go!" Darian held Deshty by the hand and pulled her up the stairs.

Deshty followed, but not before she turned around to find Flesh was still on the floor.

The Battle for Hollow House

The monster made no attempt to chase them. Instead of anger blazing from his eyes, he was looking at the hole with a sad longing. *How strange,* Deshty thought. She paused to get her breath once they were back in her room.

"That was weird, wasn't it?" she said.

"I've never been more scared of anything in my entire life!" Darian wiped the dust off his clothes.

"I don't know ... something doesn't feel right. Flesh didn't even try to get up from the floor. Why did the portal push him out like that?"

"How do you know the portal did that? Maybe Flesh came out and hurt himself doing it," Darian said.

"But it looked like the portal was the one in charge. Like it rejected Flesh."

"Does that mean the portal will also spit out the books if it wants to?" Darian asked.

"I suppose …" a dejected Deshty realised.

"What should we do now then?" Darian said.

A pounding headache knocked against Deshty's temple.

"I need to think," she said.

"I'm going to sit with Mum and Dad for a bit," Darian said, shaking.

Deshty stepped out of the house for some fresh air. She walked a little, deep in thought, until she reached the front gate. She lifted the latch and stepped out.

Behind her, the house stirred. Okay, *shadows* stirred, but it felt like it was the whole house. She stood outside the gate and sat down, trying desperately to make sense of what she'd seen in the basement, when a woman walked by the gate. It was the first time Deshty had seen anyone venturing this close to Hollow House before.

"Good morning," she greeted Deshty before glancing behind her at the house. "It's true then – someone finally bought this place. I never thought I'd see the day."

Deshty didn't know what to say to that.

"You don't look very well, dear – are you okay?"

Deshty looked at the house, but again she said nothing. The old lady followed her gaze and came a little closer to her.

"Have you seen them yet? Those creatures ...?" she whispered.

Deshty looked up at the woman in surprise.

"You've seen them too?"

"Yes, once upon a time. I was curious so my friends and I snuck into the house one night. We never dared go back in."

"Please help us – how do we get rid of them?"

"I wouldn't know." She shook her head. "They've been there so long now, maybe they don't want to go. That's what happens when you become too attached to things."

The thought of the monsters never leaving made Deshty's skin crawl.

"I'm sorry I can't be of more help. Good luck to you." The lady walked off and Deshty trudged back into the house. Something the lady had said niggled at Deshty for the rest of the morning, but she couldn't put her finger on what.

After Deshty had showered and changed into fresh clothes, she picked up her dirty trousers from the floor. The picture Darian had found in the basement fell from the pocket. She must have put it there when she'd seen Flesh. Deshty stared at it again and something in her brain finally clicked. The house seemed to be filled with Flesh and Bones' stuff — what if she and Darian dumped all of their memories down the portal? Then they would have no reason to stay in the house.

"Darian! Darian!" she yelled down the stairs.

"Keep it down!" her mum yelled back from the kitchen.

"What is it?" Darian ran into the hallway, looking up at her.

"I know what we need to do," Deshty said.

"What's that?"

She explained the new plan to Darian. They would collect all the sentimental things that belonged to Flesh and Bones and get rid of them, hoping it would make them disappear too.

Darian gawped at her.

"But there's so much stuff in the house. What do we throw away exactly?"

"Do you remember when the guest room flooded in our old house?"

"Yes, but what's that got to do with it?" Darian said.

"The first thing Mum and Dad saved were the photo albums, so I think we should find as many old pictures as we can and get rid of them first."

"I'll grab a couple of bin bags," Darian said.

Farewell

The sun had set by the time they managed to fill the bags up with the monsters' memories.

"Where should we dump all this?" Darian asked as they stood in the hallway by the front door.

Mum walked past and stared at the bags in their hands.

"Don't tell me you two are finally tidying up?" She smiled.

Deshty nodded.

"The bins are outside – you can throw all that in there," Mum said, but Deshty thought it was still going to be too close to the house. She couldn't risk the monsters finding it.

"I'm going up for a shower and your dad is in bed – he's not feeling too well," Mum announced.

As soon as Deshty heard the shower turning on, she noticed a shadow slip past them.

"Did you see that?" Deshty asked.

Darian's eyes nearly popped out of his skull. He was pointing behind her with his jaw wide open. She turned slowly and Flesh was standing within centimetres of her, stretching his hand out. He grabbed the bag full of photos from her. Darian gripped the last remaining bag with both hands.

"Run!" Deshty shouted. They tried to go up the stairs, but Bones was waiting for them by the landing, forcing them to retreat. Flesh appeared next to Bones, backing them down into the basement. There was no other direction to go in.

"Don't lose that bag!" Deshty shouted.

As the monstrous pair got closer, Deshty searched around her frantically for any route of escape, but Flesh dived for the bag in Darian's hand.

"Get in there, quick!" Deshty pushed her brother into the basement.

They ran down the stairs and tried to find something to hide behind, but the door burst open. At the same time the portal began to emerge from the ground.

"They've got us now," Darian whispered, his eyes shiny like he was on the verge of tears. Deshty edged closer to the portal, but with a speed that she had never seen before, Bones came down the steps in a blur and snatched the bag from Darian's hand. They wrestled for it until the bag broke, spilling the contents onto the floor.

The pictures flew towards the portal, the ground somehow sucking everything up as it shook, like dozens of mini earthquakes at once. Flesh and Bones froze for a moment; it seemed even they were surprised by this.

Deshty steadied herself by grabbing onto Darian. As Bones came striding towards her, she stuck her foot out and he fell into the hole. Knowing he would come flying back out any minute, Deshty tried to run, but Flesh grabbed both her and Darian by their clothes. The ground continued to shake, and Deshty could hear the faint cry of Mum and Dad calling for them.

Then, to Deshty's surprise, the strangest thing occurred. Bones did not materialise again, like she'd expected. Flesh noticed too because his grip loosened around both her and Darian – until he let go of them completely.

Deshty and Darian ran up the stairs, but Flesh did not follow them. Deshty couldn't help but pause at the top.

"What are you doing?" Darian hissed at her from the door.

"One second ..." Deshty moved a couple of steps down and caught sight of a smiling Flesh. It wasn't a creepy smile, like the one he gave her in the garden, but gentle and soft.

A single black tear rolled from his eye, thick and clumpy. Deshty took another few steps, until she was standing right in front of Flesh. The fear she'd felt earlier had disappeared as quickly as Bones had.

"All this time, if only we'd known that was all the portal needed …" Flesh spoke quietly.

"What's going on?" Darian said behind her. "What does he mean by that?"

Was Flesh crying because Bones hadn't come back from the portal? Deshty had originally thought the portal was how Flesh and Bones were able to come in and out of the house so easily but staring at Flesh now, Deshty realised she was wrong.

Flesh turned to them, still holding the bag that he'd taken from Deshty. He dropped it on the floor and walked over to them.

"Thank you," he croaked, drawing closer to Deshty and Darian. "You found the way to open the portal. All we needed to do was take our memories with us! We can return home now to the rest of our family."

"Where is your home?" Deshty dared to ask.

"Home? It's nothing like here! We have deep craters to run around in, gigantic trees that drip with delicious sticky sap and the best beetles anyone has ever tasted." Flesh licked his lips and rubbed his belly.

Taken back by the sudden emotion, Deshty and Darian leaned in to console Flesh.

"Will you come back here?" Darian asked.

Flesh laughed.

"Impossible! Once I go through that portal, there is no returning. Hollow House is yours now."

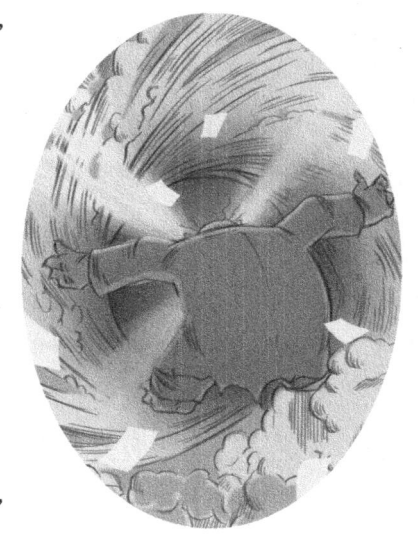

A stunned Deshty looked at Darian as Flesh turned and jumped down the hole, vanishing in a split-second.

The shaking stopped and just before the portal closed up again, it spat out Deshty's suitcase and all their missing clothes and toys, brand new, as if they had never been destroyed. Deshty and Darian looked on in disbelief as the cracks in the ground began to vanish.

"What just happened?" Darian asked his twin.

"I think we all wanted the same thing in the end — for them to return to their real home," Deshty said.

"Why didn't the portal spit them out again?"

"Because they took their memories with them this time," Deshty said.

"We did it then? We got rid of the house monsters!"

"We did!" Deshty said and they high fived each other, jumping up and down in happiness.

The basement door opened, and Mum and Dad ran down the steps.

"For goodness' sake, you two! We've already told you not to come here. I think we just had an earthquake, so come on, out now in case another one hits," Mum said.

Deshty wanted to tell them it was no earthquake, but instead she just followed Mum and Dad up the stairs.

"You're unusually smiley," Dad said, looking at Darian. "Are you getting used to our new home now?"

"Yes." Darian nodded, his smile bigger than ever. Deshty grinned back. They were going to be happy in this new home – now that it was truly theirs. She hoped Flesh and Bones were happy too, somewhere far away, in the Land of Monsters ...

Now answer the questions …

1 What did Deshty see when she first looked in the basement on page 7?

2 Why was Darian angry on page 16?

3 Darian rubbed his temple on page 21. What does 'temple' mean in this context?

4 Why did Darian bury his face in his hands on page 33?

5 'Before it disappeared inside, it grinned at Deshty – an evil, malicious grin' (page 39). What does 'malicious' mean?

6 What happened when Deshty and Darian went to the library in the town?

7 What did you think would happen when they filled the hole in the basement with books?

8 How did you feel when you found out that Flesh and Bones just wanted to go home?